AKRON-CANTON
FOOTBALL HERITAGE

D1709554

ROUTE 21 AND INTERSTATE 77 are the Tigris and the Euphrates Rivers of today's modern football. Route 21 leads to the Tigers, and Interstate 77 will send any football fan into euphoria. Interstate 77 connects Cleveland, Akron, and Canton, the hottest bed of football in the history of mankind. Route 21 connects Massillon to this group. To the people of this region, the Tigris and the Euphrates are the start of human civilization, but Route 21 and Interstate 77 are the start of life.

On the front cover: Mike Adamle is seen diving in to the end zone for a touchdown. (Photograph courtesy of the Cleveland Press Collection from Cleveland State University.)

On the back cover: This photograph depicts the press box at the Pro Football Hall of Fame Field at Fawcett Stadium. (Photograph courtesy of the Maroon collection.)

Cover background: This photograph captures the Akron Zips in action against Louisiana Tech in 1968. (Photograph courtesy of the University of Akron Archives.)

AKRON-CANTON
FOOTBALL HERITAGE

Thomas Maroon, Margaret Maroon, and Craig Holbert

ARCADIA
PUBLISHING

To our families, for their love and support and

for putting up with our football obsession.

CONTENTS

ACKNOWLEDGMENTS

THIS BOOK WOULD NOT be possible without the generous contributions of many individuals and organizations. The authors wish to specifically thank Ryan Nissan of the Philadelphia Eagles, Jared Puffer of the New England Patriots, and Patrick Herb of the Kansas City Chiefs. The authors also wish to thank William Barrow of Cleveland State University, Gary Harwood of Kent State University, the University of Akron, Canton-Central Catholic High School, and the Canton Legends. From the Browns Backers of Canton, the authors wish to thank Chuck Schuster, Bob Ferne, and Shawn Cassidy (hopefully we will see a Browns championship in our lifetime). And finally, the authors thank Jeff Ruetsche and the Arcadia Publishing team for their help and guidance in making our dream come true.

INTRODUCTION

IN THE EARLY DAYS of football, most players took the field simply for the love of the game. Many players transferred from team to team within the same week, if not within the same day, just to play again. Few of them thought of this as a career. They did not have safety equipment and played with a much wider ball that looked more like a "pigskin." Many of them had no idea that they were creating the way for super athletes and the hoopla associated with the game today.

Despite the majority of players participating for the thrills, the excitement of smashing an opponent, and for the opportunity to show their shear strength in front of a crowd, Billy Heston from Michigan is noted as being the first real holdout. Every owner refused to offer a contract to him because of his high demands. Collusion was not a factor during this era nor was there a players' union. After sitting out an entire season, Heston played for Canton at the outrageous figure of $600 per season. On the very first play in Chicago, he broke his leg and never played again.

Though Heston may not have been popular to everyone, the most loved football family graced the field early in football history. Their last name was Nesser, and there were seven brothers who played the game. The Nessers included Al, Charlie, Frank, Fred, John, Phil, and Ted. Al Nesser made a name for himself in the Akron area, while most of his brothers played for the Columbus Panhandlers. Panhandlers was a term given to railroad workers of the day. The Nessers came with a history of being railroad workers who used to hurry through their lunch to get in a game of football. Al played with the likes of Charley Copley, Fritz Pollard, and Jim Thorpe. He was the last player to play without a mandatory helmet. Fans would fill the stands when they knew the Nessers were in town. Many teams had blackout rules in Ohio to prevent players from outshining their game and starting another game at a nearby venue. The owners feared that these superstars and others would take advantage of owners' advertisements and upstage them with another game at the same time. Owners were not pleased with the possibility of losses at the gate.

Some meaningful football firsts took place in Akron and Canton. The first player ever traded was from Akron. The first franchise move caused the Canton Bulldogs to head to Cleveland. The game first hit the Akron area in a serious way in 1890 when the freshmen of Buchtel College lost to the upperclassmen by a score of 30-8. The following year, Buchtel lost its first game against another college (Reserve) by a score of 22-6. The first coach for Buchtel, Frank Cook of the Cleveland Athletic Club, came to the school in 1892. Central High School organized a team that same year and played the Buchtel freshmen. Teams, ages, and abilities were not usually considered. In 1893, John W. Heisman (for whom the Heisman Trophy is named) took over for the Buchtel College Hilltoppers and became their first full-time paid coach. While local games between Akron and Canton schools and athletic clubs were being held during this time, attempts at forming a national football league were not being made in 1902–1903. A few of the noncollegiate teams did not have a coach whereas others had two or more. Different articles at the time would list different players as the coach of the same team. Akron had one of those teams. The head coaches were listed as Elgie Tobin, Al Nesser, and Fritz Pollard (the first African American coach and a 2005 hall of fame inductee). It seemed as if there were so many first-year teams and coaches that came and went; anyone could have a team, and it may or may not have been recorded. A win counted as a win regardless of the opponent's record or skills. The big game was the college game at that time. The point system was different. In the early days, dropkicks were routine, but have not really been seen in the game for many years until Doug Flutie successfully converted one in 2005.

The Massillon Tigers, then an amateur team, noticed the strength of the Pittsburgh players and hired four of them to play in their last game of the season against Akron (1903); thus began Massillon's football tradition. It was also during this time that football popularity shifted from Pennsylvania to Ohio. Massillon continued fielding strong teams from 1904 to 1906, winning the Ohio League Championship in all three years. The Massillon team was also responsible for the first "recognized" forward pass completion on October 27, 1906, between George "Peggy" Parratt and Dan "Bullet" Riley. Knute Rockne has also been credited with the innovation of the forward pass. In 1905, the first documented Canton team played Massillon for the Ohio League Championship in 1905 and 1906, losing to them twice.

From 1908 to 1913, the Akron Indians had a reputation of being more like a college team than that of an athletic club. For example, they liked throwing the ball as opposed to running. The Indians won the city title in 1909 (6-2 over the Eastend Blues) and in 1913 (30-0 over Coleman's Indians). They tied for the city title in 1908 (0-0 against the Akron Tigers). The Indians were also successful on the state level, winning the state professional title in 1909 (12-9 over Shelby Blues Athletic Club) and the state championship in 1912 (20-0 over Shelby Blues Athletic Club).

Soon football started to take shape. Its organization was mostly started by Lester H. Higgins, who was a former president of Citizens Savings Association and a founder of the Council of Retarded Children of Stark County. Even with football organizing itself, some teams such as West Virginia did not have a team name, while occasionally some teams would have the same names as others. Hammond and Akron each had a team called the Pros. One story claims that in 1919 Frank Nied took over the Akron Indians and named them the Akron Pros. Another story claims that the Akron Pros were named as such in 1920 after the Akron Burkhardts, which held the name of a famous local family of brewers. In 1919, the league was comprised of 12 teams that included Akron, Canton, Massillon, Cleveland, and surrounding teams reaching as far as West Virginia, New York, Michigan, and the outskirts of Ohio.

In 1920, the American Professional Football Association (APFA) was formed in an attempt to play by the same set of rules. The 1920 Akron Pros were the only undefeated team in the new league's inaugural season and were awarded the 1920 championship based on a win-loss percentage. That same year, Massillon had a powerful team but did not have the $100 to join the league.

In 1922, the APFA changed its name to the National Football League. The league consisted of 18 teams that year but has substantially grown into the 32 teams existing today. Though many of the rules have changed, it is still one of the most popular games on earth. This fantastic journey that started over a century ago with Akron and Canton at its center is now celebrated around the world.

THE NATIONAL
FOOTBALL LEAGUE

THE AKRON-CANTON area gave birth to the game of football as fans know it today and has not stopped contributing since. Football fans of this area are some of the most knowledgeable fans of the game in the world. Nearly all walks of life carry football in their hearts and wear their team colors on their sleeves. It is this very attitude and way of life that has created a right of passage from one generation to the next. This tradition has helped to create a plethora of talented players from the area and launch them into a professional career. Even though there is not an NFL franchise in the Akron-Canton area per se, the love and pride instilled in the hearts of these passionate people help to make the game what it is today. The great players of the past with the tremendously skilled athletes of today are creating a game for the future gridiron stars from this area in the professional arena of tomorrow.

Football's beginnings took place in Akron with Buchtel College and in Canton with the start of the NFL. Football experienced many growing pains through its infancy but overcame them with the desire to make this game work as an organized and professional league. From the time period of roughly 1920 through 1940, the game evolved with some minor changes but took much stock in players such as Jim Thorpe, who helped to put the game on the map. With baseball holding the forefront, football needed to take a major-league maturing leap of modernization. Again football turned to this area and looked to Massillon, where it found Paul Brown. Brown was an innovator of the modernization of football. Football no longer saw players just show up to play. Practices, exercises, and more complex play patterns began to take shape. As he led the Cleveland Browns to multiple championships, a forced merger between the AFL and the NFL became a necessity. Football had become a rousing success on a national level.

Football is constantly growing and maturing even today. The NFL has become the ultimate goal of all players at any level. One thing that makes the NFL so great is its continuous attention to this area. Since Paul Brown, all eras of football have seen great stars emerge from Akron, Canton, and Youngstown. The 1960s saw great superstars such as Len Dawson grace the field. In the 1970s, players such as Larry Csonka and Jack Lambert truly represented this region in a way it deserves. From the 1980s with Bernie Kosar and Ron Jaworski to today with Antonio Gates and Charlie Frye, the list is seemingly endless. Stars of the recent past and stars of the future will continue to make Akron-Canton the hotbed of the NFL.

WHILE JIM THORPE IS MOST FAMOUS for winning the decathlon and pentathlon in the 1912 Olympics, his sports career did not end there, as seen by his shrine in the Football Hall of Fame. In 1915, general manager Jack Cusack of the Canton Bulldogs signed Thorpe as a halfback for $250 a game. With Thorpe, the Bulldogs won the "unofficial" football championship in 1916, 1917, and 1919. More importantly, his name recognition brought so much publicity to the league that when the NFL was formed in 1920, Thorpe was elected league president. He continued playing football with various teams through 1928 (1915–1920, 1926 Canton; 1921 Cleveland; 1922–1923 Oorang; 1924 Rock Island; 1925 New York/Rock Island; 1928 Chicago Cardinals), where he not only ran the ball but could pass, block, and kick as well. He was inducted into the Football Hall of Fame in 1963. (Photograph courtesy of the Cleveland Press Collection from Cleveland State University.)

GUY CHAMBERLIN (second from left) was recruited by Jim Thorpe as an end for the Canton Bulldogs in 1919. After playing for the Decatur and Chicago Staleys in 1920 and 1921, respectively, he returned to the Bulldogs in 1922 as both player and coach. With Chamberlin, the Bulldogs went undefeated in 1922 and 1923 and won the NFL championship. When the Canton Bulldogs were sold and moved to Cleveland in 1924, Chamberlin went with them and promptly won another championship. In 1925, Chamberlin moved on to the Frankford Yellowjackets, where he won another championship in 1926. In 1927, Chamberlin went to the Chicago Cardinals as a player only. He returned the following year to the Cardinals as a coach only in his last year in the NFL. His six-year coaching record was 58-16-7, for an impressive .759 winning percentage. Chamberlin was inducted into the Football Hall of Fame in 1965, as seen in this photograph with the rest of the induction class. (Photograph courtesy of the Cleveland Press Collection from Cleveland State University.)

Table 1: Akron Pros' Record from 1920 to 1926

Year	Record	Conference	Place
1920*	8-0-3	APFA	1st
1921	8-3-1	APFA	3rd
1922	3-5-2	NFL	10th
1923	1-6-0	NFL	15th
1924	2-6-0	NFL	13th
1925	4-2-2	NFL	5th
1926**	1-4-3	NFL	16th

*Champion of league
**Pros changed their name to the Akron Indians in 1926

Table 2: Canton Bulldogs' Record from 1916 to 1926

Year	Record	Conference	Place
1916*	9-0-1	Ohio League	1st
1917*	Not recorded	Ohio League	1st
1919*	Not recorded	Ohio League	1st
1920	7-4-2	APFA	8th
1921	5-2-3	APFA	4th
1922*	10-0-2	NFL	1st
1923*	11-0-1	NFL	1st
1924**	Did not play		
1925	4-4-0	NFL	11th
1926	1-9-3	NFL	20th

*Champion of league
**Bulldogs moved to Cleveland; awarded a new franchise in 1925, keeping the name Bulldogs

THE CLEVELAND BULLDOGS were formed in 1924 when Sam Deutsch (owner of the Cleveland Indians football team) purchased the Canton Bulldogs after the 1923 season to the outrage of Canton fans. In their inaugural year, the Bulldogs had a record of 7-1-1 and won the NFL championship with a win over the Chicago Bears 23-0. The following year, Deutsch sold the franchise to Herb Brandt, and the team staggered to a 5-8-1 finish. Brandt suspended football operations in 1926, but the Bulldogs returned for one more season in 1927 before finally folding, ending with an 8-4-1 record. (Photograph courtesy of the Cleveland Press Collection from Cleveland State University.)

WHEN THE ALL-AMERICAN FOOTBALL CONFERENCE (AAFC) folded in 1949, the Cleveland Browns (in dark jerseys playing against the Los Angeles Dons in 1948) merged with the NFL in 1950 while the Dons were paired with the San Francisco 49ers. (Photograph courtesy of the Cleveland Press Collection from Cleveland State University.)

THE 1948 BROWNS from left to right are Vince Marotta, Bob Brugge, Ara Parseghian, Tommy James, Warren Lahr, and Dean Sensanbaugher. Marotta of Mount Union was drafted by the St. Louis Cardinals (baseball) and the Browns (football). Brugge was a sixth-round pick of the Bears. Parseghian is an Akron native who played with the Browns from 1947 to 1948 before injuries forced him to retire. With his playing career over, Parseghian turned to coaching, where he had his greatest success at Notre Dame (two national championships and three bowl games from 1964 to 1974). James was born in Canton and played under Paul Brown at Massillon, Ohio State, and Cleveland. Originally drafted by the Detroit Lions in 1947 as a defensive back, James helped Cleveland win the AAFC in 1948 and 1949, as well as the NFL championship in 1950, 1954, and 1955. Lahr, drafted by Pittsburgh in 1947 from Case Western Reserve University, had 45 interceptions from 1950 to 1959, second on the all-time list (the first being Thom Darden). Sensanbaugher of Midvale, Ohio, played college football for Ohio State and Army. He holds the longest kickoff return record for the Buckeyes. (Photograph courtesy of the Cleveland Press Collection from Cleveland State University.)

THE NATIONAL FOOTBALL LEAGUE

MARION MOTLEY (front left) was born in Leesburg, Georgia, on June 5, 1920. He played high school football at McKinley (where Paul Brown first became familiar with him from "next door" Massillon Washington High School) and college football at South Carolina State and Nevada. Motley joined the Cleveland Browns in 1946 primarily as a fullback but also played linebacker and pass blocker. He is the all-time rushing leader in the AAFC as well as holding the record for yards per carry (5.7). His success was not limited to the AAFC; he was the leading NFL rusher in 1950, the year the Browns joined the league. His 18.4 average yards from scrimmage is still a Browns record (against Pittsburgh on October 29, 1950). Motley played for the Browns up to and including 1953, followed by Pittsburgh in 1955 for one season before retiring. He played in the 1951 Pro Bowl and was elected to the Football Hall of Fame in 1968. (Photograph courtesy of the Cleveland Press Collection from Cleveland State University.)

HORACE GILLOM (above, punting the football; below, pictured on the right with Bill Willis at left) attended Massillon Washington High School, followed by college at the Ohio State University. He entered the army in 1941 and afterward attended the University of Nevada for one year before joining the Browns in 1947. Gillom was primarily a punter; however, he also played the end position on both offense and defense. As a punter, he holds the Browns' record for the top three longest punts (80 yards vs. New York Giants November 28, 1954; 75 yards vs. Pittsburgh Steelers October 20 1950; and [tied for third] 73 yards vs. Washington Redskins October 26, 1952). Gillom also holds the Browns' record for the longest gross punting average (43.8 yards per punt) and is second in total punt yards (21,207 yards) and gross average yards in a season. He played for the Browns from 1947 to 1956, making the Pro Bowl in 1952. (Photographs courtesy of the Cleveland Press Collection from Cleveland State University.)

TONY ADAMLE (seen going after Pittsburgh Steelers end Elbie Nickel in a 1951 football game wearing a No. 74 white jersey) was born in Alliance, Ohio, and attended Collinwood High School (in Cleveland) and the Ohio State University. He joined the Browns in 1947 and had the distinction of being a member of a championship team in his first five years with them (1947–1951). Adamle was an all-pro linebacker, making all-league honors in 1951 and being elected to the 1951 and 1952 Pro Bowl. Following the 1951 season, Adamle retired from football to attend medical school. However, in 1954, Paul Brown persuaded him to rejoin the Browns for one more year to replace injured linebacker Tommy Thompson. The move was successful, as the Browns won the 1954 NFL championship with Adamle's help. After that season, Adamle retired for good and went on to have a successful 40-year medical career, which included being the team doctor for 30 years at Kent State University. (Photograph courtesy of the Cleveland Press Collection from Cleveland State University.)

PAUL EUGENE BROWN (center), born September 7, 1908, in Norwalk, Ohio, is considered one of the greatest coaches in NFL history. He brought championships wherever he coached, whether it be high school, college, or at the professional level. Brown changed the way football teams were coached by using his intellect rather than his brawn. For example, he used classroom skills (such as notebooks, films, and intelligence tests) to evaluate and teach his players. Furthermore, he designed complex passing patterns as well as complex defensive strategies to counteract both the running and passing game. His career winning percentage with the Browns (.759) is the best in the club's history. (Photograph courtesy of the Cleveland Press Collection from Cleveland State University.)

DEEMED TOO SMALL TO PLAY FOOTBALL at the school of his first choice (the Ohio State University), Brown transferred to Miami University of Ohio, where he played quarterback. He graduated from Miami University in 1930 with a bachelor of arts degree in education and later returned to the Ohio State University to get his master of arts degree in education in 1940. (Photograph courtesy of the Cleveland Press Collection from Cleveland State University.)

PAUL BROWN'S COACHING CAREER started at the Naval Academy's Severn School in Severna Park, Maryland, in 1930. After two years at Severn (with a 16-1-1 coaching record) and a short detour at law school, Brown returned to his home town of Massillon in 1932 to coach his high school alma mater: the Massillon Washington High Tigers (as seen in this picture). During his nine-year tenure at Washington, Brown had an amazing 80-8-2 coaching record. He won six consecutive state championships (1935–1940) and won the national championship in 1935, 1936, 1939, and 1940. Brown's success led to the building of a new high school football stadium bearing his name with a capacity of 20,000. (Photograph courtesy of the Cleveland Press Collection from Cleveland State University.)

AFTER NINE YEARS at Massillon Washington High, Brown returned to Ohio State in 1941, this time as head coach of the Ohio State Buckeyes. In his three-year career at Ohio State, Brown had an 18-8-1 coaching record and led the Buckeyes to a Rose Bowl victory and national championship in 1942. With World War II in full effect, Brown left Ohio State in 1944 and enlisted in the navy, where he coached the Great Lakes Naval Station football team for two years (15-5-2). In 1946, Brown joined the Cleveland Browns as its vice president, general manager, and head coach, and the team was named after Brown himself based on the results of a poll from the Cleveland Plain Dealer. The Browns that year went 12-2 and won the All-American Football Conference championship (as seen in this picture). (Photograph courtesy of the Cleveland Press Collection from Cleveland State University.)

PAUL BROWN (center), surrounded by quarterback Otto Graham (left) and tackle Lou Rymkus, won his second All-American Football Conference championship with the Cleveland Browns in 1947 via a 14-3 win over the New York Yankees. Brown's recipe for success consisted of switching players' positions based on his own talent evaluation. For example, he switched Otto Graham from running back to quarterback, with it resulting in the Browns playing in 10 straight championship games (AAFC and NFL combined) starting in 1946. He was also one of the first coaches to recruit African American players like Bill Willis and Marion Motley, who played high school football at McKinley in Canton. (Photograph courtesy of the Cleveland Press Collection from Cleveland State University.)

UNDER BROWN (seen here in suit and hat watching the last play of a Cleveland Browns game in 1947), the Cleveland Browns went on to win the All-American Football Conference championship in 1948 and 1949. Both wins were against Buffalo (49-7 in 1948, when they went undefeated and won 15 straight games, and 31-21 in 1949). Brown's career record in the All-American Football Conference is an impressive 52-4-3. (Photograph courtesy of the Cleveland Press Collection from Cleveland State University.)

AKRON-CANTON FOOTBALL HERITAGE

THE CLEVELAND BROWNS entered the NFL in 1950 (seen here with Paul Brown at far right with coat, suit, and hat) with the merger of the AAFC and NFL. In their NFL debut on September 16, 1950, the Browns beat the defending NFL champion Philadelphia Eagles 35-10. They went on to have a record of 10-2 and won their first of three NFL championships with a victory over the Los Angeles Rams (formerly of Cleveland) 30-28 on Lou Groza's last-minute field goal. The Browns appeared in each NFL championship game from then until 1955, winning the championship in 1954 (56-10 over the Detroit Lions) and 1955 (38-14 over the Los Angeles Rams). The Browns appeared in one more championship game with Brown as coach (1957 loss to the Detroit Lions 59-14). Overall, Brown's career record with the Browns was 167-53-8, with only one losing season between 1946 and 1963 (1956, 5-7). (Photograph courtesy of the Cleveland Press Collection from Cleveland State University.)

ON JANUARY 9, 1963, after 17 seasons with the Cleveland Browns, Brown was fired by new owner Art Modell in an attempt to gain more control over the team. For the first time in 30 years, Brown was not a football coach. In 1968, Brown returned to football as part owner, general manager, and coach of the Cincinnati Bengals of the American Football League. In his tenure, the Bengals made the playoffs three times, and Brown was elected Coach of the Year in 1969 and 1973. In 1976, Brown retired from coaching the Bengals but remained with the team in other capacities, where he saw his team go to the Super Bowl twice, both times losing to San Francisco. He was president of the Bengals up until his death in 1991. (Photograph courtesy of the Cleveland Press Collection from Cleveland State University.)

PAUL BROWN (top left with Lou "The Toe" Groza) was truly a remarkable coach and human being. His career coaching record was an astonishing 351-134-16. He won four AAFC championships and three NFL championships. He was inducted into the Football Hall of Fame in 1967, based only on his career with the Cleveland Browns. His final resting place is where it all began: Massillon (below). Fans will truly never see the likes of him again. (Top photograph courtesy of the Cleveland Press Collection from Cleveland State University.)

DANTE LAVELLI (No. 56) was born in Hudson, Ohio, on February 23, 1923, and was originally a quarterback at Hudson High School, where the field is currently named after him. At the Ohio State University, coach Paul Brown switched him to receiver after his freshman year. In 1946, he was drafted by the Cleveland Browns, where he led the league in receptions and won All-AAFC honors in his first year. More importantly, he caught the winning touchdown pass against the New York Yankees in the first AAFC championship game. (Photograph courtesy of the Cleveland Press Collection from Cleveland State University.)

DANTE LAVELLI (center in picture to the left) continued having success with the Browns when they moved to the NFL in 1950 until he retired in 1956. He was elected to three of the first five Pro Bowls and caught 11 passes and scored two touchdowns in the 1950 championship game against the Los Angeles Rams (Browns won 30-28). He was one of quarterback Otto Graham's favorite targets (as seen in photograph below from a 1952 game), catching all but 20 of his 386 receptions from him. Lavelli was inducted into the Football Hall of Fame in 1975. (Photographs courtesy of the Cleveland Press Collection from Cleveland State University.)

CLEVELAND BROWNS DEFENSIVE END Jim Houston (center, No. 82) was born in Massillon on November 3, 1937, and attended high school in his hometown at Massillon Washington High School. He had a storied college career at the Ohio State University, where he played both offense (wide receiver and blocker) and defense (tackle) and helped them win a share of the national championship in 1957 (Auburn). In fact, Houston played so much football that he averaged an astonishing 51 minutes a game. He was voted All-American and All–Big Ten twice, as well as MVP of his team twice at two positions (offense and defense). Houston was drafted by the Cleveland Browns in 1960 and played his first 3 years at defensive end before being switched to linebacker for his remaining 10 years with the Browns. He had a total of 14 interceptions, was voted to the Pro Bowl in 1965, 1966, 1970, and 1971, and helped the Browns win the NFL championship in 1964. In 2006, Houston was inducted into the College Football Hall of Fame. (Photograph courtesy of the Cleveland Press Collection from Cleveland State University.)

ALREADY WINNERS OF THE EASTERN DIVISION of the NFL, the Browns did not know who they would be playing for the NFL championship: Baltimore or Green Bay. Thus, to be on the safe side, Jim Kanicki (left) and Jim Houston (center) wore signs to beat each team, while Bill Glass (right) wore a Jim Brown for President sign. (Photograph courtesy of the Cleveland Press Collection from Cleveland State University.)

LIN HOUSTON (far left in the right photograph, far right in photograph below) was born in Carbonale, Illinois, on January 11, 1921, and played under Paul Brown in high school (Massillon Washington High School), college (the Ohio State University), and professionally (Cleveland Browns from 1946 to 1953). Houston was known on the Browns as "Mr. Perfection" due to his "perfect" play on the offensive line. (Photographs courtesy of the Cleveland Press Collection from Cleveland State University.)

LARRY CSONKA (seen here diving over the goal line versus the New York Jets on November 19, 1972) was born on December 25, 1946, in Stow, Ohio, and attended Syracuse University. The Miami Dolphins drafted him with their number-one pick in 1968, and he played for them for seven seasons (1968–1974). His best season was in 1972, when he rushed for 1,117 yards and helped Miami go undefeated and win Super Bowl VIII. He was elected MVP of that Super Bowl with 145 yards rushing and two touchdowns (Super Bowl records at that time). After playing one year (1975) with the Memphis Southmen of the World Football League, he returned to the NFL with the New York Giants from 1976 to 1978. In 1979, he rejoined his old team for one final year, setting career records in total touchdowns (13) and rushing touchdowns (12). He was elected to the Football Hall of Fame in 1987. (Photograph courtesy of the Cleveland Press Collection from Cleveland State University.)

MIKE ADAMLE (No. 34, seen here scoring a touchdown for Northwestern University in 1970) is the son of Cleveland Browns great Tony Adamle. Born in Kent, Ohio, Adamle attended Northwestern University from 1967 to 1971 and was elected All-American fullback and MVP of the Big Ten in his senior year. He was a fourth-round draft pick of the Kansas City Chiefs in 1971. From 1973 to 1974, Adamle played for the New York Jets, and from 1975 to 1977, he played for the Chicago Bears. Following his retirement in 1977 (due to a water-skiing accident), Adamle made a name for himself in broadcasting. Some of his jobs have included working at NBC Sports from 1977 to 1983, hosting *American Gladiators* from 1989 to 1994, and serving as sports director of WBBM Channel 2 in Chicago in 2002. (Photograph courtesy of the Cleveland Press Collection from Cleveland State University.)

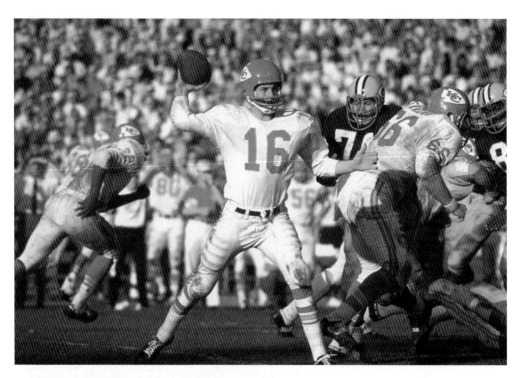

LEN DAWSON (above) is one of the most famous players in the history of football. Leonard Dawson was born in Alliance, Ohio, on June 20, 1935. He attended high school in Alliance, where the school presently has a football field named after him (left). After high school, Dawson went to Purdue University and is a member of the Boilermakers Hall of Fame. Dawson was a No. 1 draft choice of the 1957 Pittsburgh Steelers. After being mostly a backup quarterback with Pittsburgh and the Cleveland Browns, he went to the Dallas Texans, who became the Kansas City Chiefs in 1963 (Above, courtesy of the Kansas City Chiefs.)

LEN DAWSON won two AFL titles prior to the institution of the Super Bowl. In 1962, after leaving the Browns for the Texans, Dawson became the AFL Player of the Year. In addition to holding many awards and records, he made two Super Bowl appearances. In Super Bowl I, his Kansas City Chiefs, coached by the legendary Hank Stram, lost to the Green Bay Packers. Dawson had a fabulous MVP performance in Super Bowl IV as the Chiefs defeated the Minnesota Vikings. Len Dawson threw for a total of over 16 miles in his 19-year career. That is just about the distance from downtown Alliance to the Professional Football Hall of Fame in Canton. (Photograph courtesy of the Kansas City Chiefs.)

ALAN PAGE was born on August 7, 1945, in Canton and attended Canton Central Catholic High School, graduating in 1963. He attended the University of Notre Dame, where he was an All-American and helped the Fighting Irish win a national championship in 1966. From Notre Dame, Page was drafted by the Minnesota Vikings as a defensive tackle and spent most of his career with the "Purple People Eaters." He also played for NFC Central rival the Chicago Bears toward the end of his career. He played in four Super Bowls and 236 straight games. In 1971, while with the Vikings, Page was the first defensive player to receive the MVP Award in NFL history. He was inducted into the Pro Football Hall of Fame in his home city of Canton in 1988 and had Alan Page Drive named after him in 1989. While playing football and being a superstar with the Vikings, Alan found the time to attend and graduate from the University of Minnesota School of Law. After football, Page became a Minnesota Supreme Court justice. (Photograph courtesy of Canton Central Catholic High School.)

LARRY POOLE (at Kent State in the picture to the right and as a Cleveland Brown in picture below) was born in Akron on July 31, 1952. He attended Garfield High School in Akron and went to college at Kent State University, where he was arguably the best running back Kent ever had. Poole holds Kent records in career rushing yards (2,668 yards), career touchdowns (38), touchdowns in a season (18), points scored in a season (108), and career points (228). In 1973, he was second in the country with 18 touchdowns and 108 points. Furthermore, Poole was elected All–Mid-American Conference first team in 1973–1974, as well as honorable mention Associated Press All-American in 1974. He was inducted into the Kent State Athletics Hall of Fame in 1983 (Right, photograph courtesy of Kent State University; below, photograph courtesy of the Cleveland Press Collection from Cleveland State University.)

In 1975, LARRY POOLE (far left in photograph above, left in the photograph to the left) was drafted in the ninth round by the Cleveland Browns. He played for the Browns for three seasons, with his most productive season yardage-wise in 1976 (356 yards rushing) and touchdown-wise in 1977 (four touchdowns). In 1978, Poole played one more year of football as a kick returner with the Houston Oilers before retiring. (Photographs courtesy of the Cleveland Press Collection from Cleveland State University.)

JOHN "JACK" LAMBERT was born on July 8, 1952, in Mantua, Ohio. He attended Crestwood High School and Kent State University, where he holds many records. Lambert was a second-round pick of the Pittsburgh Steelers and played his entire career for them. In 1974, he was the Defensive Rookie of the Year and in 1976 was the Defensive Player of the Year. The defense propelled the Steelers to their first Super Bowl win in 1975 over the Minnesota Vikings in Super Bowl IX. The next year, the defense was a factor again as they rose to the occasion to defeat the Dallas Cowboys. Three Super Bowls later, the Steelers won two more Super Bowls in a row, defeating the Dallas Cowboys again, then defeating the Los Angeles Rams, thus creating the phrase "win one for the thumb." Pittsburgh accomplished this in 2006. (Photograph courtesy of Kent State University.)

STARING AT JACK LAMBERT leaves very little to the imagination of the pain he inflicted upon unsuspecting offensive players. Whether looking at the grimace he wore, sporting only a handful of teeth that only a hockey player would admire, one can only surmise the pleasure he felt inflicting pain. He played during an era when players played for the love of the game. Lambert played in many famous games, including the Immaculate Reception and "Turkey" Joe Jones's pile driving of Terry Bradshaw. He clearly is an elite hall of famer. (Photographs courtesy of Kent State University.)

JAY BROPHY (seen in this picture as the head coach of the Canton Legends on opening day) attended Akron Buchtel High School and played for the Miami Hurricanes in college as a tremendously talented linebacker. He won a national championship his senior year as a captain of the team and was drafted by the Miami Dolphins as second-round pick. He then appeared in the Super Bowl his rookie year and nearly held a coveted record of playing for a national championship one year and a Super Bowl championship the next. In 1987, Brophy played for the New York Jets. He loves working with young people and devotes much time to football. Jay Brophy coached Akron St. Vincent–St. Mary star LeBron James on the gridiron. He also played on a Hurricanes team with Boardman phenom Bernie Kosar. Though Kosar is best known for leading the Cleveland Browns and starring opposite Doug Flutie, then of Boston College, Kosar did not play for the Dolphins at the same time Brophy was there.

ANDREW HARMON was born in Centerville, Ohio, and attended Kent State University. He was drafted by the Philadelphia Eagles in 1991 and played his entire career there (1991–1997). The action photographs (No. 91, white jersey) show Harmon in pursuit of another sack against foes like the New York Giants and the Pittsburgh Steelers (Left, photograph courtesy of Ed Mahan and the Philadelphia Eagles; below, photograph courtesy of the Philadelphia Eagles.)

BORN JAMIESON READER in Washington, D.C., on May 4, 1974, this fullback played one season with the Philadelphia Eagles. He attended the University of Akron, where he joins a long list of great professional players. The University of Akron, formerly known as Buchtel College, has produced such players as John Heisman, who lends his name to the trophy given to the best college football player each year; Jason Taylor of the Miami Dolphins; Charlie Frye of the Cleveland Browns; Victor Green of the New England Patriots, New York Jets, and the New Orleans Saints; Ralph Waldsmith of the Canton Bulldogs when they won back-to-back championships; and many others. Akron's mascot, Zippy the Kangaroo, would be proud. (Right, photograph courtesy of the Philadelphia Eagles; below, photograph courtesy of Brian Killian and the Philadelphia Eagles.)

BORN ON APRIL 16, 1952, the son of former Detroit Lions back Steve Belichick, Bill has come close to being at home in the Canton area. Bill was not even 60 miles away from his future home when he was a former head coach of the Cleveland Browns. Currently, Bill is the only coach in NFL history to win three Super Bowls in a four-year span. His New England Patriots nearly made it to the big show again in the 2005 season. In time, he will find a home in Canton as an inductee. As the sign on the wall of Fawcett Stadium next door to the hall of fame indicates, the hall of fame will call. (Left, photograph courtesy of the New England Patriots.)

THE NATIONAL FOOTBALL LEAGUE

MICHAEL VRABEL was born on August 14, 1975, in Akron and attended Walsh Jesuit High School in Stow, Ohio. Other noteworthy Walsh graduates around the country include Doug Flutie, Dan Fouts, Vince Lombardi, Gino Marchetti, Ollie Matson, Ken O'Brien, Joe Paterno, Pete Rozelle, Don Shula, and Paul Tagliabue, as well as many others. After Walsh, Vrabel went to the Ohio State University, where he holds many records, including sacks. Following his fabled history with the Buckeyes, he was drafted by the Pittsburgh Steelers in 1997 and went to the Patriots in 2001. Vrabel has eight touchdown receptions despite the fact that he is a fearsome linebacker. Two of those touchdown receptions were of the super variety. The first one was in Super Bowl XXXVIII against the Carolina Panthers and the second came one year later in Super Bowl XXXIX against the Philadelphia Eagles. Vrabel has three Super Bowl rings. (Photograph courtesy of the New England Patriots.)

Josh McDaniels was born April 22, 1976, and is the current offensive coordinator and former quarterback coach of the New England Patriots. He is the youngest current offensive coordinator in the NFL. McDaniels has also served the Patriots as a scout and a defensive coach. He was born in Canton and attended John Carroll in Cleveland. Nick Caserio also played football at John Carroll and is now the director of personnel for the Patriots. John Carroll has turned out other championship members such as the likes of Don Shula, London Fletcher, and Carl Taseff just to name a few. (Photograph courtesy of the New England Patriots.)

Born on June 18, 1980, in Detroit, Michigan, Antonio Gates attended Michigan State, Eastern Michigan, the College of Sequoias in California, and Kent State University. He worked with Dean Pees and Nick Saban. He led the Kent State Golden Flashes to back-to-back Mid-American Conference (MAC) titles and helped them reach the Elite Eight in the NCAA Basketball Tournament. He has been one of the best tight ends the game has seen in a long time and appears to be destined to return to Ohio as a member of the hall of fame. Antonio Gates has been a two-time Pro Bowl selection and has made the trip to Honolulu to face some of the league's best. (Photograph courtesy of Kent State University.)

KEN WALTER is the left-footed punter in this photograph, punting against the Akron Zips. Walter was born on August 15, 1972. He held the record for the Carolina Panthers of most punts inside the 20-yard line, at 86, until it was eclipsed by Todd Sauerbrun. Walter was originally drafted by Carolina and played for the New England Patriots as well as the Seattle Seahawks. In Super Bowl XXXVIII, Walter faced his former Panthers and won a Super Bowl with the Patriots. He has won two Super Bowl rings from his seasons with the Patriots. He has punted over 500 times for well over 20,000 yards. (Photograph courtesy of Kent State University.)

THE NATIONAL FOOTBALL LEAGUE

JOSHUA CRIBBS was born on June 9, 1983, and attended Kent State University. He has become an explosive wide receiver and kick returner for the Cleveland Browns. His abilities electrify the crowd every time he touches the ball. Cribbs was the starting quarterback at Kent State and fits into the same mold of many other great MAC players. At one time, Cribbs and Akron Zips quarterback Charlie Frye were opposing quarterbacks. Today they are both young superstars for the Cleveland Browns. Cribbs became the first freshman in NCAA history to run and pass for more than 1,000 yards in the same season. His athleticism has allowed him to play multiple positions at the NFL level. (Photograph courtesy of Kent State University.)

IS THERE MORE to life than just football? That is a difficult answer for most football fans in this area. Though there are many chapters of Cleveland Browns Backers across the country, none of them are more serious, knowledgeable, or more willing to share their knowledge and love of the game than the Canton Browns Backers. This picture includes a few members and their bright orange bus that can be seen traversing Interstate 77 to catch the Browns home games. (Photograph courtesy of the Canton Browns Backers.)

2

OTHER PROFESSIONAL
FOOTBALL LEAGUES

PROFESSIONAL FOOTBALL does not just come in the form of the NFL. Many arena leagues and other outdoor leagues have sprung up all over the United States, Canada, and Europe. Though many of the leagues are now defunct, this area has played a large part in their development, which directly and indirectly changed the shape of the game as it is known today. Some players have become household names, and others may not be known by anyone other than their own mother. Akron, Kent State, and many local high schools have sent numerous players into these leagues. Some players are in these leagues hoping to catch the eyes of NFL scouts. Others are in these leagues by direction of the NFL to finish rehab or to fine tune the skills necessary to become a force in the big show.

The Richfield Coliseum in Summit County used to house indoor football games. The coliseum was built in 1973 and had an official address of 2923 Streetsboro Road, Richfield, Ohio 44286. It was a $36 million project that opened with Frank Sinatra. After that, it housed many sporting teams such as the Cleveland Thunderbolts, the Cleveland Barons, the Cleveland Cavaliers, the Cleveland Crunch, the Cleveland Crusaders, the Cleveland Force, and the Cleveland Lumberjacks.

Randy Gradishar, a member of the Orange Crush, is from Warren, Ohio. He is best known for playing football for 10 years with the Denver Broncos, appearing in Super Bowl XII, and for his college playing days at Ohio State. He was the 1978 Defensive Player of the Year. However, the World Football League wanted him, too. Gradishar was the 26th overall pick by the New York Stars, who eventually became the Charlotte Hornets, in 1974. Gerald Tinker of Kent was the 62nd overall pick and went to Washington/Baltimore, which never fielded a team as such. Many NFL players such as Larry Csonka joined the World Football League.

Though they may not be well known, many area players have made their mark in arena football all over the country with teams like the Cleveland Thunderbolts and the Canton Legends. They have also played for minor-league football teams such as the Akron Redpeppers, the Akron Jaguars, the Massillon Bengals, and the Mahoning Valley Panthers as well. The list is seemingly endless. Whether a player makes it to the NFL, which is the ultimate goal, or ends up being an obscure statistic in a player listing, football is in their blood. It would be ludicrous to any one of these players not to play the game regardless of the level.

THIS TEAM THAT PLAYED their home games at the Akron Rubber Bowl had a very unusual story. The Vulcans played in the Continental Football League in 1967. The league was a minor-league football league that intended to compete with the NFL and the AFL. The Vulcans' head coach was the great Doak Walker. Their starting kicker was Tom Furlong, who was an Irish soccer player that spent a preseason with the Atlanta Falcons prior to blowing out his knee. Stanley Rudolph Sczurek, formerly of Cleveland Benedictine and the Cleveland Browns, was a starting linebacker. The owner of the Vulcans took the gate receipts and was captured by the FBI. The Akron police shut down the team before it barely started.

Cleveland Thunderbolts

As an arena team, the Cleveland Thunderbolts averaged just over 7,400 fans per game. They had an 8-37 record, which includes one playoff loss to the Orlando Predators in 1992. After posting a record of 0-10 in 1991 in Columbus, the Thunderbolts moved to Richfield, Ohio, where they were known as the Cleveland Thunderbolts for the next three years. They spent the next three years in Richfield. They were quarterbacked by Major Harris of West Virginia, who had a fantastic college career. Eric Wilkerson of Kent played for the Pittsburgh Steelers in 1989, and as a wide receiver and defensive back for the Cleveland Thunderbolts in 1993. Darryl Gard of Akron spent all four years with the Thunderbolts as a wide receiver and defensive back.

THE CANTON LEGENDS inaugural game was on April 17, 2005. The Raleigh Rebels defeated the Legends by a score of 50-28. This was a fast-paced game at the Canton Civic Center on Market Avenue, the former home of the indoor soccer team the Canton Invaders. As the game wore on, the Legends made it closer than the score might have indicated. Canton was led by Mount Union quarterback Rob Adamson. Andrew Haines owns the Legends and started the Atlantic Indoor Football League. Canton was chosen because of the legendary history of football in the area. The entry fee for a team was $35,000.

OPENING JITTERS take place just about an hour prior to game time. Owner Andrew Haines (center right, in suit) checks to see how things are progressing prior to the fans' arrival.

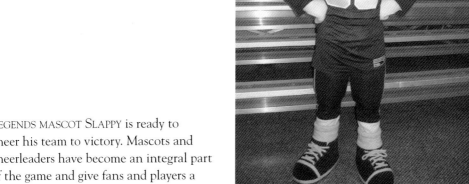

LEGENDS MASCOT SLAPPY is ready to cheer his team to victory. Mascots and cheerleaders have become an integral part of the game and give fans and players a rallying point.

JIM BALLARD is the offensive coordinator of the Canton Legends. Ballard played quarterback at Cuyahoga Falls High School but is most noted for leading Mount Union to their first Division III national championship in 1993. He has played football at many levels, including the NFL, NFL Europe, CFL, XFL, and the Arena Football League. As a member of the Scottish Claymores, Ballard led the team to a World Bowl Championship in 1996 and is a member of their hall of fame. In between playing for many teams, Ballard found time to coach quarterbacks at Cuyahoga Falls (2001–2004), Alliance (1996, 1998), and Mount Union (1994–1995).

COACH RON JONES found much success in the tough Suburban League with Copley and Wadsworth. He poses here with his son Bobby Jones, who starts at tight end and defensive end for the Canton Legends. Bobby also played a season with the New York Giants as a defensive end and long snapper. Besides playing at Wadsworth, Bobby also played for legendary coach Joe Paterno at Penn State.

LAVEL BAILEY (No. 88 of the Raleigh Rebels) was a former University of Akron football star. Many players in arena leagues throughout the country are focusing on NFL Europe and the NFL itself. Some of the players are working with teams during rehab. Others are playing hoping to catch on with a team as they have an open forum to display their skills and speed in this fast-paced game.

JOHN MCRAE was a player with the Akron Buchtel Griffins and won two state championships under coach Tim Flossie. Buchtel has been no stranger to great football. They have seen the likes of Rickey Powers and others. While at Buchtel, McRae participated in the last Turkey Day Game in Akron, as the Griffins defeated the Garfield Rams in a fourth-quarter nail-biter. After high school, he played for the University of Pittsburgh as a middle and outside linebacker under coach Paul Hackett, formerly of the New York Jets. While at Pitt, McRae participated in the "backyard brawl," recording 17 tackles against West Virginia. Later McRae teamed up with Tim Flossie and Jay Brophy to help Akron Central-Hower High School in their final season of play (2005). In this picture, McRae is working and helping out the Canton Legends. Recently McRae had a son named John Jr. who someday may follow in his father's footsteps. McRae spends much time coaching football and helping young people.

OTHER PROFESSIONAL FOOTBALL LEAGUES

3

The University
of Akron

Tracing its roots back to Buchtel College in 1870, the University of Akron has over 24,000 students today. It fluctuates with Kent State as being the third-largest school in Ohio. Against Youngstown State, the University of Akron has posted a record of 18-18-2. Against their archrival Kent State, Akron holds a record of 27-19-2. Overall the Zippers are 468-442-36 in their storied football history. Akron boasts having John Heisman coach Buchtel College in 1893 and 1894. Heisman also quarterbacked the team in a game. The university brought the Dallas Cowboys cheerleaders to a nationally televised game at the Rubber Bowl when Gerry Faust first arrived. Akron won the Knute Rockne Bowl for Division II schools in 1976.

In 2005, Akron won their first MAC championship, gaining a birth into the Motor City Bowl to face the Memphis Tigers. The Zips made a fine showing but lost to the Tigers by a score of 38-31. The Motor City Bowl was played on Ford Field in Detroit. It was marked with a unique call toward the end of the game. The Akron nose tackle swatted at the ball as it was snapped from center, causing a fumble which Akron recovered. After a review of the play, though the Akron player never touched the ball, the Akron nose tackle was considered encroaching the neutral zone, and the ball went back to Memphis to eventually end the game. The guaranteed payout was $750,000. Not only did this game end on a last-second thriller, it was preceded by a last-second thrilling win over Northern Illinois to win the MAC on literally a prayer by wide receiver Domenik Hixon. Hixon came back from an injury during the game to score the winning touchdown reception from quarterback Luke Getsy.

Coach J. D. Brookhart has done a remarkable job with this team. Brookhart was a former nonpaid assistant with the Denver Broncos and an assistant coach with the Pittsburgh Panthers. He played for the Colorado State Rams and was cut as a free agent with the Los Angeles Rams. Akron has had their share of great coaches, such as Jim Dennison and Gerry Faust. The Zips' home is the Akron Rubber Bowl, which has gone back and forth between the city and the university. The Rubber Bowl overlooks Derby Downs (home of the All-American Soap Box Derby) and the Goodyear Airdock which used to house the blimp. The name for the mascot, Zippy (a kangaroo), was officially adopted May 1, 1953, and has become one of the most loved mascots in all of sports. The kangaroo was chosen because of its uniqueness, speed, agility, and determination. The school colors are blue and gold. Some of the former Akron players in professional football today include Dwight Smith (Tampa Bay), Butchie Washington (Hamilton Tiger Cats, CFL), and Jason Taylor (Miami), just to name a few.

THE UNIVERSITY OF AKRON has fielded football teams since 1891, competing as the Buchtel College Hilltoppers from 1891 to 1913. There were a number of highlights in the early days, including a win over the Ohio State Buckeyes by a score of 12-6 during the 1894 season. (Photograph courtesy of the University of Akron Archives.)

A GROUP OF PROUD University of Akron students hold a Buchtel College team photograph featuring John Heisman (in the University of Pennsylvania shirt on the far right). The Cleveland native coached Buchtel College during the 1893 and 1894 seasons before going on to have his name immortalized on the trophy that bears his name. (Photograph courtesy of the University of Akron Archives.)

THE FUTURE University of Akron Zips competed as Buchtel College for 23 years. Old Buchtel went 44-43-3 during those years, creating a football frenzy in the area. The above photograph is a pennant from the Buchtel College era. (Photograph courtesy of the University of Akron Archives.)

HERE ARE THE PLAYERS from Buchtel College's last team of 1913. Team captain Ralph Waldsmith led coach Frank Haggerty's team to a 3-4 mark in its last season before the name change. (Photograph courtesy of the University of Akron Archives.)

THIS COLLAGE OF PHOTOGRAPHS represents the stars of the University of Akron's first season after the change in name from Buchtel College. Frank Haggerty's crew went 4-4-1, a season marred by a 75-6 loss to Michigan State. (Photograph courtesy of the University of Akron Archives.)

ON DECEMBER 28, 1950, the Mayflower Hotel in Akron hosted a reunion of coach Frank Haggerty's 1910 Buchtel College team that went 7-2. In this photograph, three of that team's veterans hearken back to their season of glory. Haggerty coached at Buchtel from 1910 to 1914, its first season as the University of Akron. (Photograph courtesy of the University of Akron Archives.)

HERE 1910 TEAM CAPTAIN Lee Jackson sets up to pass. Jackson, who lettered during the 1909–1911 seasons, was a very influential member of the Akron community in later years, serving as an executive at Firestone and having Lee Jackson Field at the university named in his honor. (Photograph courtesy of the University of Akron Archives.)

TWO OTHER IMPORTANT FIGURES from Akron were present at the reunion, university president Hezzleton Simmons (left) and publisher John S. Knight. A building on campus was named after Simmons and a building in downtown Akron bears the name of Knight. Lee Jackson is holding the game ball from the 1910 3-0 defeat of Oberlin College. (Photograph courtesy of the University of Akron Archives.)

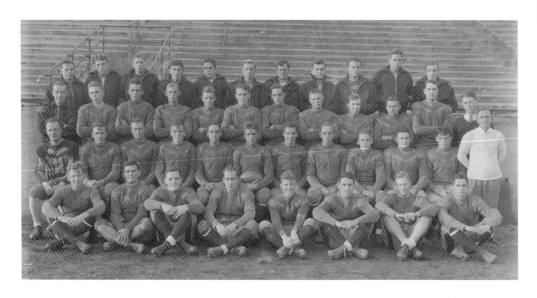

HOWARD "RED" BLAIR coached Akron from 1927 to 1935, going 42-30-5 highlighted by a 9-1 season in 1929. Akron's captain that season was Harold Frye, who would remain Akron football's most notable Frye until Charlie Frye's arrival in 2001. Shown here is the University of Akron football team around 1932. (Photograph courtesy of the University of Akron Archives.)

COACH BLAIR is joined in this photograph by one of his predecessors, Fred Sefton. Sefton coached Akron to a 34-33-4 mark between 1915 and 1923, including a 6-1-1 record in 1919. (Photograph courtesy of the University of Akron Archives.)

MY HOW TIMES HAVE CHANGED! Akron's 1937 foes ranged from 2005 Division I-A bowl participant Toledo to the West Virginia State Teachers College. Akron had a very successful season in 1937, defeating the Rockets and the Teachers on their way to a 7-2 record. (Photograph courtesy of the University of Akron Archives.)

1937 HOME SCHEDULE

SEPT. 25	W. VA. STATE TEACHERS
OCT. 2	WAYNE UNIVERSITY
OCT. 9	GENEVA COLLEGE
OCT. 23	BALDWIN-WALLACE
OCT. 30	JOHN CARROLL
NOV. 6	DAVIS & ELKINS
NOV. 13	ILLINOIS WESLEYAN

GAMES AWAY

OCT. 16—TOLEDO	AT TOLEDO
NOV. 20—XAVIER	AT CINCINNATI

ORIGINALLY HAILING FROM GEORGIA, Martin Chapman went on to star for the University of Akron in spite of not having played high school football. Like many others during the World War II time period, Chapman had his playing career interrupted during the conflict. Chapman lettered during the 1941, 1942, and 1946 seasons. (Photograph courtesy of the University of Akron Archives.)

IN WHAT WAS A VERY SPARSELY attended game in 1958, Akron and Baldwin-Wallace slug it out. With the field a quagmire, the season finale ended in a 0-0 tie. (Photograph courtesy of the University of Akron Archives.)

ONE OF AKRON'S most noteworthy seasons was 1968, which ended with a 7-3-1 record and an appearance in the Grantland Rice Bowl in Murfreesboro, Tennessee. The Zips came up short in the game, losing to the Terry Bradshaw–led Louisiana Tech squad 33-13. (Photograph courtesy of the University of Akron Archives.)

AKRON FOLLOWED UP the successful 1968 campaign by doing even better in 1969. They finished with a 9-1 mark and a final ranking of third in the Associated Press college Division II poll. Head coach Gordon Larson went 74-33-5 between 1961 and 1972. Ironically Larson was a Kent State alumnus. (Photograph courtesy of the University of Akron Archives.)

THE WINNINGEST COACH in Akron history is Jim Dennison, who led the Zips to an 80-62-2 mark between 1973 and 1985, including postseason appearances in 1976 and 1985. After leaving Akron, Dennison moved on to Canton's Walsh University, where his success has continued. (Photograph courtesy of the University of Akron Archives.)

AKRON CITY SCHOOLS have produced a number of college stars and NFL veterans over the years, including Dave Brown, Jim Lash, Ricky Powers, Charles Gladman, Nate Winfield, and Antonio Pittman, just to name a few. Don Buckey starred at Kenmore in the early 1970s along with his twin brother, Dave, before going on to play for Kent State product Lou Holtz at North Carolina State and then with the New York Jets.

AKRON TAILBACK Doug Lewis sprints to daylight against Kent State in this 1989 40-7 win over the Kent State Golden Flashes. Lewis led the Zips in rushing in both 1988 and 1989, topping out at 763 yards during the 1989 campaign. (Photograph courtesy of the University of Akron Archives.)

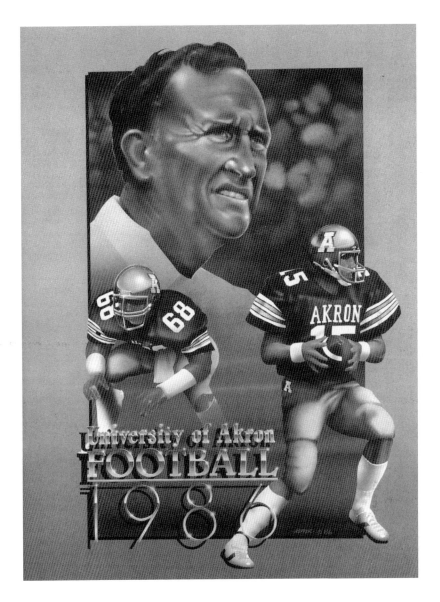

GERRY FAUST started his football career as the quarterback and strong safety of the University of Dayton, where he was a three-time letterman. He started his coaching career at Cincinnati Moeller High School, where he won five state championships and had a won-loss record of 174-17-2 between 1963 and 1980. Faust then went to the Fighting Irish of Notre Dame, where he compiled another winning record (30-26-1) with two bowl appearances and a bowl victory. He continued to make football a part of his life when he took over the reigns at the University of Akron in 1986. Much fanfare followed him, including a nationally televised game featuring the Dallas Cowboy cheerleaders. Faust coached the likes of players such as former St. Vincent–St. Mary standout Frank Stams while he was at the University of Notre Dame. He spent nine seasons at Akron, compiling a 43-53-3 record. (Photograph courtesy of the University of Akron Archives.)

GERRY FAUST is in the National High School Football Hall of Fame and has implemented many programs into the high school ranks. Faust also plays an integral part in athletics for the University of Akron. Nearly five teams worth of players who were coached by Faust entered the NFL. His religious faith and dedication to helping young people made him one of the greatest coaches in football history. As seen in this picture, Faust makes friends with a young recruit named Tommy.

PERHAPS THE MOST stellar athlete to ever come out of the University of Akron is Jason Taylor. The future All-Pro defensive end for the Miami Dolphins starred for the Zips between 1993 and 1996, earning All-MAC honors in 1996. As a member of the Miami Dolphins (73rd pick in 1997), he is the team's all-time leader in sacks, fumble recoveries, and fumble recoveries for a touchdown. In 2004, Taylor started the Jason Taylor Foundation, which benefits children in southern Florida. (Photograph courtesy of the University of Akron Archives.)

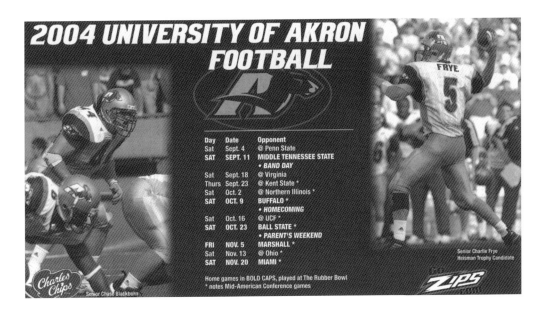

UNIVERSITY OF AKRON and future Cleveland Brown's quarterback Charlie Frye attended high school in Willard, Ohio, setting 17 school records, including pass completions (482), passing yards (6,209), and passing touchdowns (54). In his senior year, Frye led his team to the state's playoffs and was named Northwest Ohio's District Player of the Year. As quarterback for the University of Akron from 2001 to 2004, Frye passed for 11,049 yards (11,478 total yards of offense) and had 87 total touchdowns. Furthermore, he set an impressive 54 school records, including total passing yards and pass completions in a season. In 2005, Frye was drafted in the third round by the Cleveland Browns (67th overall pick). In his rookie year, Frye played in seven games (starting in five) and completed 98 out of 165 passes for 1,002 yards. He had five total touchdowns (four passing, one rushing). (Top photograph courtesy of the University of Akron Archives.)

WITH HIS record-setting performance in 2004, Charlie Frye generated attention for college football's highest reward: the Heisman Trophy. The University of Akron helped his cause by distributing promotional buttons celebrating the achievements of Frye, as well as former coach John Heisman. (Photograph courtesy of the University of Akron Archives.)

ONE OF THE MORE unique and well-known college mascots is Akron's Zippy the kangaroo. The kangaroo was first chosen as mascot in 1953, and the current incarnation of Zippy became official in 1965. Today the phrase "Fear the Roo" can be heard all over northeastern Ohio. (Photograph courtesy of the University of Akron Archives.)

THE SITE OF the University of Akron Rubber Bowl was originally a recreational center developed under the direction of B. E. Fulton in 1933 (adjacent to the Akron Municipal Airport). In 1939, C. W. Seiberling and James Schlemmer raised $30,000 by receiving $1 from 30,000 Akron residents to convert the recreational center to a stadium. With the help of a federal grant for $516,000, the Rubber Bowl was completed on August 10, 1940. Leaving its previous home of Buchtel Field, the Akron football team played its first game at the Rubber Bowl on October 5, 1940, losing to Western Reserve 6-0. In 1973, the University of Akron received the title of the Rubber Bowl from the City of Akron and promptly started making improvements to the stadium, starting with a new lighting system. Over the years, the Rubber Bowl has received AstroPlay artificial surface, new scoreboards, and refurbished seats.

THE AKRON RUBBER BOWL presently has a capacity of 31,000, tied for the largest stadium in the Mid-American Conference (with Buffalo) and second in the state (behind the Ohio State University). The Zips have played over 300 games at the Rubber Bowl, with an overall win-loss record of 181-114-10. The Rubber Bowl hosted 19 preseason Cleveland Brown games (the last in 1973), high school playoff games, and events such as music concerts.

WHILE ATTENDING an Akron Zips football game at the Rubber Bowl, one can see Derby Downs (above), home of the All-American Soap Box Derby, and the Goodyear Airdock (below). Derby Downs was built in 1936 as a Work Progress Administration project. The course consists of three lanes (10 feet wide apiece) approximately 1,600 feet long. The race is usually held in July and is preceded by a weeklong celebration and festivities. The Goodyear Airdock was built in 1929 by the Goodyear Zeppelin Corporation. The airdock is 1,175 feet long, 325 feet wide, and 211 feet in height. With its completion, Akron became one of the leaders in zeppelin construction. Recently, the Goodyear Airdock was bought by the Lockheed Martin Corporation in 1996.

THE AKRON FIELD HOUSE of the University of Akron contains a 120-yard football field with an AstroPlay artificial surface (like that of the Rubber Bowl) and locker rooms, as well as an 8,000-square-foot conditioning center. The center also has a indoor golf facility, a 300-meter, six-lane track, and a 3,500-square-foot sports medicine center. Not far from the field house is the Akron Zips outdoor practice facility.

IN RECENT YEARS, the quality of Akron's opponents has risen, and a number of opponents with storied histories have begun to visit the Rubber Bowl. Here is Akron in action against Army (light jerseys) in October 2005. The Zips loss the game 20-0, the first time the team has been shut out at home since October 15, 1994, against Central Michigan (47-0) and their first overall shutout since September 18, 2004, against Virginia (51-0).

AGAINST ARMY, the Zips only had 44 rushing yards and 188 passing yards. Their quarterback, Luke Getsy (below, No. 16), is a junior from Munhall, Pennsylvania. A transfer student from the University of Pittsburgh, Getsy sat out his sophomore year at Akron due to NCAA rules but did not lose a year of eligibility. Getsy has done a remarkable job filling the shoes of Charlie Frye.

THE UNIVERSITY OF AKRON

AFTER FINISHING the regular 2005 season with a 6-5 record, the University of Akron won its first MAC championship, defeating Northern Illinois 31-30 in the title game at Ford Field in Detroit (scoring 21 points in the fourth quarter). On December 26, Akron returned to Detroit to face Memphis in the Motor City Bowl, their first-ever Division I bowl appearance, in front over 50,000 fans. Akron (in white) played Memphis tight in the beginning, being down 13-3 at halftime.

IN THE SECOND HALF, All-American running back DeAngelo Williams of Memphis scored two touchdowns and rushed for a game total of 238 yards in helping Memphis take a 38-17 lead with just three minutes to go in the game. However, Akron staged a late rally and scored two touchdowns in the final three minutes to decrease their deficit to only seven. A recovery of an onside kick by Memphis with less than a minute in the game preserved the victory for Memphis by a score of 38-31. Quarterback Luke Getsy of Akron set a Motor City Bowl record for passing yards (455), and wide receiver Jabari Arthur set a Motor City Bowl record for receiving yards (180, breaking the previous record set by Randy Moss).

4

KENT STATE UNIVERSITY

KENT STATE UNIVERSITY was founded in 1910. Its motto is Imagine. Kent State's nickname is the Golden Flashes, and it has the eagle as its mascot. Currently Kent has an enrollment of over 36,000 students. It is less than 15 miles from its MAC rival the Akron Zips (19-27-2 all-time record) and less than 45 minutes from the nearby Youngstown State Penguins (3-6 all-time record).

The Kent State Golden Flashes sport blue and gold colors. They have a storied football history and have seen many talented coaches and players grace their field of Dix Stadium. The battle with Akron is for the coveted Wagon Wheel. Legend has it that John R. Buchtel of Akron was looking to start another college nearby. When his wagon wheel was stuck, he started Kent State University. In 1972, Kent won its first MAC championship, which was a much-needed image boost following the 1970 Kent State shootings. The Golden Flashes were led by a strong defense that included Jack Lambert. In 1975, Kent played Bowling Green as a part of a doubleheader at old Cleveland Municipal Stadium. The main game featured Michigan and Toledo. This doubleheader was unique to college football.

One famous Kent enshrinee includes Don "The Dogfather" James. James was born in Massillon on December 31, 1932, and lettered in baseball, basketball, football, and track at Massillon before coaching the Golden Flashes to their first MAC championship in 1972. Kent has seen the likes of other great coaches such as Lou Holtz, Glen Mason, and Dean Pees. A current list of Kent State Golden Flashes in professional football includes some household names such as Joshua Cribbs (kick returner, Cleveland Browns), Antonio Gates (tight end, San Diego Chargers), head coach Nick Saban (Miami Dolphins), and Dan Goodspeed (Winneipeg Blue Bombers, CFL), just to name a few.

DIX STADIUM, home of the Kent State Golden Flashes football team, was built in 1969 and seats 30,520. The stadium is named after Robert C. Dix, who was a member of Kent State's board of trustees for more than 30 years. In 1996, permanent lights were added to the stadium, followed in 1998 by a new scoreboard and an exterior scrolling marquee. The stadium's press box is considered to be one of the elite in the Mid-American Conference, housing private loges and work space for the media and announcers. In 2005, the field's artificial turf was replaced by FieldTurf.

EUGENE BAKER was born in Monroeville, Pennsylvania, and attended Kent State University from 1995 to 1999. He is the university's all-time leader in receptions and led the entire country in receptions in 1997. In the same year, Baker was voted first-team All-Conference and third-team Football News All-American. Baker was a fifth-round draft choice of the Atlanta Falcons in 1999 and played with them until 2002. Since then, he has played with the Carolina Panthers and New England Patriots. (Photograph courtesy of Kent State University.)

GENO "JUNGLE" GIOIA was drafted by the Boston Patriots in 1960 but chose to play football for the Cleveland Bulldogs. Gioia received his bachelor's degree from Kent and his master's degree from Western Reserve University. He lettered three times in football and three times in baseball at Kent. Gioia was the captain of the Golden Flashes football team in 1956. (Photograph courtesy of Kent State University.)

JAMES CORRIGALL was born on May 7, 1946, in Barrie, Ontario, Canada. He attended Kent State on a scholarship and became the first player in school history to be named to the All-MAC team three years in a row (1967–1969). For a time, Corrigall held the all-time tackle record with 334. He was drafted by the St. Louis Cardinals in the NFL but chose to play football for the Toronto Argonauts in the CFL. He made an immediate impact as he was named Rookie of the Year. Corrigall was an All-Pro seven times. His No. 79 was retired from Kent in 1970. After leaving the CFL, Corrigall went back to Kent to be the head coach from 1994 to 1997. He holds many honors in the CFL, including his induction into the Canadian Football Hall of Fame and being named an All-Time Argo in 1997. (Photographs courtesy of Kent State University.)

DANIEL GOODSPEED was born on May 20, 1977, in Cleveland and was a great force with which to be reckoned for the Kent State Golden Flashes. His career made stops with the San Francisco 49ers for four preseason games, then to the New York Jets, the Tampa Bay Buccaneers, the Washington Redskins, and the Miami Dolphins. He is currently an offensive lineman with the Winnipeg Blue Bombers in the CFL, working to help them win the Grey Cup. (Photograph courtesy of Kent State University.)

ROBERT "BUCK" HEIN played basketball, wrestled, participated in track, and played football at Kent. Hein lettered eight times for the Golden Flashes. In 1944 and 1945, he served in the Marine Corp, where he played football for the El Toro Marines. He spent his professional football career playing for the Chicago Rockets. The Rockets were members of the AAFC from 1946 to 1948. In 1949, they were known as the Chicago Hornets. They posted an 11-40-3 record during those seasons. Three teams from that league joined the NFL. They were the Baltimore Colts, the Cleveland Browns, and the San Francisco 49ers. Hein taught and coached at Kent High School. (Photograph courtesy of Kent State University.)

Lou Holtz started his storied football career as a linebacker at Kent State, where he coached in later years. He served as an assistant at Ohio State as well as Iowa, Connecticut, South Carolina, and William and Mary. Soon he became the head coach of William and Mary and took them to their only Division I bowl appearance (1970). Holtz's winning ways continued as he took over the head coaching job at North Carolina State where they made bowl appearances. Holtz tried a short stint with the New York Jets but only went 3-10. This pushed him back to the college ranks, where he led Arkansas to multiple bowl games. Holtz moved on to be the head coach of the Minnesota Golden Gophers, who were horrendous prior to his arrival. He put them back on the map and into a bowl. He finally found a home and said he would never leave unless he was offered the head coaching position at Notre Dame. In 1986, his wish came true. (Photograph courtesy of Kent State University.)

KENT STATE UNIVERSITY

In 1986, Holtz's dream came true when he accepted the head coaching position at Notre Dame. Holtz headed up the Fighting Irish's national championship and arguably should have had two, with one of them going to the Miami Hurricanes. Holtz set many coaching records and has written excellent books. He is a motivational speaker and an inspiration to all. Not only is Holtz known for his coaching and caring of others, he is an awesome recruiter and a charitable donor. Holtz has helped those in need through a variety of charitable events. After approaching Knute Rockne's record, Lou retired. He soon came out of retirement and took over the South Carolina Gamecocks. The Gamecocks became a force with which to be reckoned. Holtz holds too many college coaching records to mention. He is currently a national television analyst. Holtz's winning ways have followed him wherever he has gone, and he is clearly one of the best to ever make his mark not only on the game but on people's lives as well. (Photograph courtesy of Kent State University.).

Don "The Dogfather" James was born in Massillon on December 31, 1932. James lettered in baseball, basketball, football, and track at Massillon. James was the head coach of Kent State from 1971 to 1974, and he led them to their first MAC championship in 1972. His coaching record at Kent State was 25-19-1. James was inducted into the College Football Hall of Fame in 1998. (Photograph courtesy of Kent State University.)

James Jones is a member of the Kent State Athletic Hall of Fame. He was drafted by and had a tryout with the Detroit Lions in 1941. He played semiprofessional ball for the El Toro Marines in 1944 and the Cherry Point Marines in 1945. Jones lettered three times for Kent State. (Photograph courtesy of Kent State University.)

KENT STATE UNIVERSITY

CHARLES "COCKY" KILBOURNE is a member of the Kent State Athletic Hall of Fame. He lettered 11 times in five different sports. One of his claims to fame is holding the record for the longest punt in Kent history (99 yards). Kilbourne also captained the 1929 and 1930 teams as well as intercepted Capital five times in a single game. (Photograph courtesy of Kent State University.)

JUD LOGAN was born on July 19, 1959, in Canton. Logan played football as a tight end for Hoover High School in Canton. Hoover is a member of the tough Federal League and holds about two decades worth of championships. Logan participated on two of these championship teams. After high school, Logan played for the Kent State Golden Flashes. He is best known for his Olympic performances in the hammer throw. Today Logan is the track and field coach at Ashland University. (Photograph courtesy of Kent State University.)

GLEN MASON was born on April 9, 1950, and is a native of New Jersey but spent time in this area as head coach of the Kent State Golden Flashes. He played football at Ohio State prior to coming to Kent as a coach. From Kent, he made a stop as head coach of the Kansas Jayhawks. Not unlike Lou Holtz making a stop at Ohio State, Kent, and Minnesota, Mason is the head coach of the Golden Gophers and has turned around the program to put them back on the map. He also spent some time with Allegheny College, Ball State, Iowa State, and Illinois and as an assistant at Ohio State under Woody Hayes. Mason has been named Coach of the Year with three teams in three different conferences. He did so with Kent in the MAC, Kansas in the Big Eight, and Minnesota in the Big Ten. He is only one of three coaches in NCAA history to accomplish this feat. (Photograph courtesy of Kent State University.)

DICK MOSTARDI lettered in both football and track during his playing days at Kent State University (1958–1960). He was elected first-team All-MAC quarterback in 1958 and made the second team in 1959. In 1960, Mostardi's teammates elected him both captain and MVP of their team. Following Kent State, Mostardi played for the Cleveland Browns, Minnesota Vikings, and Oakland Raiders from 1960 to 1962. In 1988, Mostardi was elected into the Kent State Athletic Hall of Fame. (Photograph courtesy of Kent State University.)

LUKE "BUFFALO" OWENS was born on October 9, 1933, and spent his college days at Kent State, winning five letters between track and football. Originally drafted by the Baltimore Colts, he spent his second season with the Chicago Cardinals and moved with them to St. Louis in 1960. He played from 1957 through 1965. His main position was offensive lineman, but he switched to defense when he went to the Cardinals. (Photograph courtesy of Kent State University.)

DONALD NOTTINGHAM attended Ravenna High School prior to playing football for Kent State. While at Kent, Don lettered three times and was named captain one year. He was a very productive running back and today has an award named after him: the Don Nottingham Cup, which is given to the top offensive player at the end of spring practice. He was drafted by the Baltimore Colts but spent most of his time with the Miami Dolphins. He joined the Colts the year following their first Super Bowl victory. He joined the Dolphins the year following their first Super Bowl victory as well. His next year, following the Dolphins' perfect season, Nottingham helped Miami win a Super Bowl against the Vikings. Nottingham played football for Don Shula and alongside many hall of famers. (Photograph courtesy of Kent State University.)

KENT STATE UNIVERSITY

HERB PAGE was an excellent kicker for the Kent State Golden Flashes. He was an integral part of the 1972 MAC championship team. Page received eight letters in three sports. He excelled at football, golf, and ice hockey. He was drafted by the British Columbia Lions as a place kicker following his graduation at Kent. His true skills are shown on the golf course. In 1983, he was selected by *Sports Illustrated* as the PGA Merchandiser of the Year in the public golf course category. Page was selected MAC Coach of the Year seven times and coached the Kent State University golf team to its only regional title in school history. (Photographs courtesy of Kent State University.)

GARY PINKEL was the leading receiver on the 1972 MAC championship team. The following year, he was the MVP and team captain as he led Kent to their best record in school history (9-2). From Kent, Pinkel went on to coach football at several schools and led Toledo to a MAC title with an 11-0-1 record in 1995. He reached 40 wins for the Toledo Rockets faster than any coach in school history. Under his leadership, Toledo was ranked an impressive 24th in the country. Pinkel is currently the head football coach at the University of Missouri. (Photographs courtesy of Kent State University.)

NICK SABAN was born on Halloween in 1951 in Fairmont, West Virginia, and is currently the head coach of the Miami Dolphins. He has served with other professional teams, including the Cleveland Browns and the Houston Oilers under then head coach Jerry Glanville. Saban has been no stranger to northeast Ohio. He was a defensive back for the Kent State Golden Flashes from 1970 to 1972 and played in the Tangerine Bowl for them. He also served as an assistant coach as well as the head coach of Kent. Other stops include Louisiana State University, where he won a national championship, the Naval Academy, Ohio State under Earle Bruce, Syracuse, Toledo, and West Virginia. Saban has helped to raise thousands of dollars for children's charities. (Photograph courtesy of Kent State University.)

VICTOR VRABEL played on the offensive line for Kent State from 1997 to 2001 along with such players as Brian Hallett of Norton and Kevin Jamieson and Steve Smith, both of Canton McKinley. (Photograph courtesy of Kent State University.)

MICHAEL ZELE was born on July 31, 1956, in Cleveland. He attended St. Joseph High School prior to joining Kent State. Zele had a fine career at Kent and was drafted by the Atlanta Falcons. However, his claim to fame came in 1982 when he sacked the New York Giants quarterback to set up the winning field goal. This game was the next to last game before the "Strike Season." The Strike Season brought out scab players. Some of those players made NFL rosters when the strike settled. (Photograph courtesy of Kent State University.)

5

NON–DIVISION I
COLLEGES

NOT ONLY DOES the Akron-Canton area play host to two formidable Division I schools, it also has a great tradition of schools at other levels. Those schools include Mount Union, Youngstown State, Malone, and Walsh, just to name a few. The Mount Union Purple Raiders have won eight Division III national championships and have the highest winning percentage in all of college football since 1990. They also have the distinction of holding the record for consecutive wins (55, from September 2000 to December 2003). Youngstown State was a finalist in the Division II national championship in 1979 and won the Division I-AA championship under Jim Tressel in 1991, 1993, 1994, and 1997. Famous alumni include Ron Jaworski, Jeff Wilkins, Carmen Policy, and Bob Mackie. Youngstown State alumni Al Campana played alongside Johnny Lujak, George Blanda, Sid Luckman, and Pat Summerall in his tenure with the Chicago Bears and the Chicago Cardinals. In their short history, the Malone Pioneers have captured three Mid-States Football Association (MSFA) conference championships in the 1990s. The Walsh Cavaliers under coach Jim Dennison (formerly of the University of Akron) have never had a losing season, which includes one MSFA Mid-East title in 2001. The school is also considered one of the finest fully accredited science and liberal arts Catholic schools in the country. The successes of these smaller schools further add to football lore in this area.

THE UNDISPUTED KING of Division III football in America is Alliance's Mount Union College. The Purple Raiders have won eight national titles in the last 13 years, including a 35-28 victory in the 2005 Amos Alonzo Stagg Bowl over the University of Wisconsin–Whitewater.

Mount Union head coach Larry Kehres is an alumnus himself and has been responsible for all eight championships. He has been head coach since 1986 and sports a remarkable 231-20-3 mark.

WHILE QUARTERBACK of the Mount Union Purple Raiders, Rob Adamson led his team to two Division III national championships (2001–2002) and had a win-loss record of 25-0. He was originally signed as an undrafted rookie free agent by the San Diego Chargers in 2003 but was released before the start of training camp. Adamson then signed with the Carolina Panthers in December 2003 and played for the Cologne Centurions of NFL Europe in 2004. He was the starting quarterback of the Canton Legends of the Atlantic Indoor Football League in their inaugural game.

MALONE COLLEGE was built in 1957 in Canton. Its football team (the Pioneers) has been a member of the Mid-States Football Association since 1992. The Pioneers have won three championships during that time (1995, 1996, and 1998). Shown here are the Pioneers playing Ohio Dominican College at the Football Hall of Fame Field at Fawcett Stadium in October 2005 in front of a crowd of 1,900. The Pioneers jumped out to an early 13-0 lead, but Ohio Dominican scored 27 unanswered points for a final score of 27-13. The Pioneers are led by junior quarterback Brad Reifsnyder of Canton.

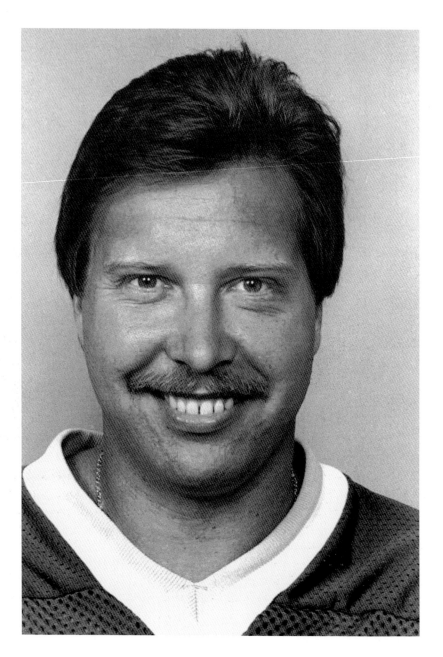

RONALD JAWORSKI, better known as "Jaws" and the "Polish Rifle," was born on March 23, 1951, in Lackawanna, New York, near Buffalo. Ron was drafted by the St. Louis Cardinals to play baseball. Deciding to attend Youngstown State University, Jaworski chose football instead. He was drafted by the Los Angeles Rams and played for Chuck Knox prior to being traded to the Philadelphia Eagles where he played under Dick Vermeil. One of his many accomplishments includes holding the record of most consecutive starts at 116 games until it was eclipsed by Brett Favre in 1999. He also was the 1980 MVP and United Press International Player of the Year. (Photograph courtesy of the Philadelphia Eagles.)

RON JAWORSKI'S accuracy and ability to dissect a defense lead him to Super Bowl XV to face the Oakland Raiders. It was the Eagles' first appearance at the big dance. Though the Eagles lost 27-10, Jaws had earned a spot among the best in Eagles history. He finished his career with a stop in Miami and a cup of coffee in Kansas City. His total passing yardage exceeded 28,000. Today Jaworski is the president of the Philadelphia Soul of the Arena Football League. One of the majority owners is Jon Bon Jovi. Jaworski is one of the most beloved analysts of the game today. He can be seen on ESPN breaking down a defense like no one else. When not involved with football, Jaworski is involved with many charitable works. (Photograph courtesy of the Philadelphia Eagles.)

JEFF WILKINS was born in Youngstown on April 19, 1979. He attended Austintown Fitch High School prior to attending Youngstown State University. This Penguins kicker was originally drafted in 1994 by the Philadelphia Eagles and played the next two years with the San Francisco 49ers (1995 and 1996). Since that time, he has been a very reliable and accurate kicker for the St. Louis Rams. He is no stranger to the Super Bowl either. He scored 11 points in one of the closest Super Bowl matches in history. The Rams defeated the Tennessee Titans by a score of 23-16. As time ran out, the Titans were within one yard of forcing the first overtime game in Super Bowl history. (Left, photograph courtesy of the Philadelphia Eagles; below, photograph courtesy of Ed Mahan and the Philadelphia Eagles.)

NON–DIVISION I COLLEGES

6

SELECTED REGIONAL

HIGH SCHOOLS

THE LOVE OF FOOTBALL in this region starts from birth, such as in Massillon where every boy receives a football and every girl a set of pom-poms. The tradition of high school football in this area is legendary. Fierce rivalries can be found from Massillon to Akron to Canton to Youngstown. Even though Friday night is normally reserved for high school football, many high school games in this area are played on Saturday. Despite Saturday traditionally being reserved for collegiate athletes across the country, high school football game attendance is not diminished one bit. In fact, it is not uncommon to see the attendance at a high school playoff game approach or exceed 20,000 spectators. Furthermore, it is expected to find the next Ohio's Mr. Football to rise on the scene from these few counties.

To the eastern side of the Akron-Canton area is Youngstown. Youngstown has played its share in producing football history. Youngstown's Cardinal Mooney High School has participated in many playoff games and has a Division IV championship in 2004. Boardman High School has produced Bernie Kosar. Warren Harding, Austintown Fitch, and Niles have all been major football producers.

In the Akron area, Barberton has produced Glenn Edward "Bo" Schembechler, who went on to give Buckeye fans fits as he led the Michigan Wolverines in many battles against Woody Hayes. George Izo was also from Barberton. Tom Tupa played for Brecksville. Antoine Winfield was a star for Garfield.

Massillon saw Chris Speilman appear on a Wheaties box while still in high school. Dan Dierdorf of Glen Oak went on to enter the hall of fame and become a television analyst after an awesome career with the St. Louis Cardinals.

There is seemingly a never-ending list of talented players from the area. It would be virtually impossible to give all of them their due justice. However, it goes without saying that after high school, many local players and coaches have gone on to have stellar collegiate and professional careers, returning or hoping to return home one day to the Pro Football Hall of Fame.

QUARTERBACK HARRY STUHLDREHER (second from left) was born in Massillon and attended Massillon Washington High School, where he met his future Notre Dame coach Knute Rockne, who himself was a player for the Canton Bulldogs between 1915 and 1919. Stuhldreher played for Notre Dame from 1922 to 1924 and was coined one of the Four Horsemen by sportswriter Grantland Rice in 1924. Rice granted the nickname (after a Notre Dame victory over Army) based on their power, skill, and intimidation over their opponents. It was in that year that Notre Dame went 10-0 and won the national championship with a victory over Stanford in the 1925 Rose Bowl (27-10). After his college playing days, Stuhldreher had a successful career in coaching college football, first with Villanova (1925–1935), then with University of Wisconsin (1936–1948), with a total record of 110-87-15. Based on his playing and coaching success, Stuhldreher was inducted into the College Football Hall of Fame in 1958. His importance to the game is further evident in the fact that he was the master of ceremonies at the groundbreaking for the Pro Football Hall of Fame in 1962. (Photograph courtesy of the Cleveland Press Collection from Cleveland State University.)

SELECTED REGIONAL HIGH SCHOOLS

SUMMIT COUNTY Sports Hall of Fame
member Horace Bell played for the University
of Minnesota when they won the 1936
national championship. He later became the
first African American to play in the All-Star
Football Game in Chicago, which matched
college all-stars against the defending NFL
champions. (Photograph courtesy of the
University of Akron Archives.)

THIS IS A PICTURE of the South High School   (Photograph courtesy of the University of
football team in Akron in the 1960s.   Akron Archives.)

MIKE BUCKNER was an all-city and all-district defensive end at East High School in the early 1960s. He went on to attain All–Big Ten honorable mention status at Northwestern and played in the North-South All-Star Game. Later he became a championship-winning coach at Buchtel High School. (Photograph courtesy of the University of Akron Archives.)

GARFIELD GREAT Thomas Lewis was a high school standout who attained all-city, all-district, and all-state honors at wide receiver. In three years, he had 120 receptions and 14 touchdowns. He next went on to a stellar career at the University of Indiana and played with the New York Giants from 1994 to 1997. (Photograph courtesy of the University of Akron Archives.)

MASSILLON WASHINGTON HIGH SCHOOL (seen in the photograph above in 1927) has a rich tradition of football dating back to 1894. The Washington Tigers have won 23 state championships (the most of any school in Ohio) and nine national championships (the most in the nation). From Paul Brown (for whom their stadium, seen below, is named) to Chris Spielman, Massillon has produced numerous football legends. Hollywood is even interested in their story; the Tigers' 1999 football season was the subject of a documentary called *Go Tigers!* released nationally in 2001 by writer and director Kenneth A. Carlson, a Massillon native. (Above, photograph courtesy of the Cleveland Press Collection from Cleveland State University.)

ROBERT COMMINGS (above, right) coached Washington High School in Massillon from 1969 to 1973 and had a career 43-6-2 record. With Commings, the Tigers won the state championship in 1970 and were ranked second in the nation that same year. He led the team to an 8-1-1 record in 1973 (left) before leaving the team to coach his alma mater Iowa University. In five years at Iowa, Commings complied an 18-37 record. He was fired after the 1978 season and in 1980 returned to high school coaching at GlenOak. Commings coached GlenOak for 10 years (1980–1991) to a 76-4-1 record. He turned the team over to his son Bob Jr. in 1991 after being diagnosed with cancer, passing away six months later. In 2002, Commings was 1 of 15 men inducted in the inaugural class of the Stark County High School Football Hall of Fame. (Photographs courtesy of the Cleveland Press Collection from Cleveland State University.)

THE CANTON MCKINLEY High
School Bulldogs have been
playing football since 1894. Their
total win-loss record is 739-304
(.709 winning percentage). The
Bulldogs have won 12 state
football championships (the last
one being in 1998) and were
runner-up in 2004. They play their
home games at the Pro Football
Hall of Fame Field at Fawcett
Stadium and practice at Don Scott
Field, both located on the hall of
fame grounds. Famous Bulldog
alumni include Marion Motley,
Wayne Fontes, and Mike Doss.

DON SCOTT FIELD, along with the Pro Football
Hall of Fame Stadium at Fawcett Stadium, is
the home of the Canton McKinley Bulldogs
and the Timken Trojans. The field was named
after Don Scott, a student and athlete at
Canton McKinley High School in the 1930s.
He was a two-time All-American quarterback
at the Ohio State University (1939 and 1940).
Although drafted in the first round to play
football by the Chicago Bears in 1941, Scott
instead joined the military. Scott died in 1943
during pilot training in England.

GARFIELD vs. HOBAN

ST. VINCENT vs. EAST

25¢

RUBBER BOWL
SEPT. 18, 1970

FROM 1963 TO 1978, other major powerhouses in Ohio included Alliance, Canton McKinley, Massillon, Niles, Steubenville, and Warren Harding who formed the All-American Conference. This conference was deemed one of the greatest high school football divisions ever assembled. The goal of its creators was to determine which school truly had the best team in Ohio and most likely the entire United States. Many of these teams played only the best high schools in the nation and could argue they had the best team themselves. In 1963, the league started with Massillon winning the conference but Niles winning the state championship. This league connected Youngstown to Canton in a bond of football that is still prevalent today. Even though the league sadly came to an end in 1978, it was of such grandeur no one who witnessed it will ever forget. Throughout the years, significant high school regional games have been played at the University of Akron Rubber Bowl. This 1970 doubleheader featured perennial Akron powerhouse Garfield and LeBron James future alma mater St. Vincent–St. Mary for the price of 25¢. (Photograph courtesy of the University of Akron Archives.)

MARCHING BANDS have been entertaining high school football fans since before the 1900s. Copley High School has been known for having one of the best bands in the area. They are seen above marching at the end of the first half against Tallmadge. School bands and cheering squads add to the football tradition, with many winning state and national championships of their own.

THIS AREA OF THE COUNTRY is home to some of the best football fans in the world. Everyone wants to be involved in the game at every level, as seen above on a Friday night in Copley.

AS SEEN IN THIS PICTURE, Delone Carter leads Copley to another winning season, trying to win the Suburban League championship. Carter transferred from Archbishop Hoban High School to Copley, where he became one of the best running backs in the country. He became an Ohio's Mr. Football. Carter will be attending Jim Brown's old alma mater Syracuse to be an Orangeman.

THE FIRST SCOREBOARD was utilized prior to 1900. Today most scoreboards are electronic as seen above. This scoreboard can be seen from Route 21 and Ridgewood Road.

TODAY ST. VINCENT–ST. MARY High School is known more for its basketball history with the likes of Jerome Lane and LeBron James than for its football history. James played football for the Fighting Irish and did well. However, St. Vincent–St. Mary has had many great players such as Frank Stams. The team has won the state championship in 1972, 1981, 1982, and 1988. In 2005, their football field was named and dedicated after former football coach John Cistone, who led the team to a 207-115-6 record from 1965 to 1996.

LOGAN RIFE is a very talented Archbishop Hoban Knight fullback who has a unique distinction of blocking for two Mr. Ohio running backs: Tyrell Sutton and Delone Carter (who transferred from Hoban to Copley). Tyrell's brother Tony (also of Hoban) holds multiple records for the Wooster Fighting Scots, including rushing touchdowns in a season (2004 and 2003), total offensive yards, rushing attempts in a season (2004 and 2003), rushing yards in as season (2004, 2003, and 2002), and many others. Tyrell went on to become a leading rusher for the Northwestern Wildcats in 2005, where he had a record-setting season of 1,474 yards as a freshman. He was named freshmen All-American by the Football Writers Association of America and *The Sporting News*, as well as the Big Ten Freshmen of the Year.

SELECTED REGIONAL HIGH SCHOOLS

7

THE PRO FOOTBALL
HALL OF FAME

THE PRO FOOTBALL HALL OF FAME is located at 2121 George Halas Drive Northwest, Canton, Ohio 44708. It is open every day with the exception of Christmas. August is a very busy month in Canton. The opening kickoff and events are a sight to see.

Induction into the hall of fame is decided by the hall of fame board of selectors. The board is made up of one representative from each NFL franchise, a representative from the Pro Football Writers Association, and six at-large representatives (total of 39). A player must be retired five years before being nominated, while nonplayers (with the exception of coaches) can still be employed in the NFL to be nominated. Anyone can nominate a player or nonplayer to the hall of fame just by contacting the board itself. On the day before the Super Bowl, the board meets to select the inductees, with the bylaws calling for three to six inductees per year. The nominee is elected if he receives 80 percent of the vote of those present.

The class of 2006 includes Troy Aikman, Harry Carson, John Madden, Warren Moon, Reggie White, and Rayfield Wright. The hall of fame celebration is a weeklong event that is one of the most exciting and festive kickoffs to any sporting event in the world. The enshrinees take part in the festivities all week long. Local television stations show NFL Films highlights during the week as well as the parade. The parade has marching bands, floats and collectible convertibles carrying the enshrined players, and the queen of the festival and her court. There are 65 hopeful contestants who try to win the right to be the festival queen. The parade route has golden football helmets painted on the street. Market Avenue is closed for a festival of food, drink, and bands. There are rib cook-offs, celebrities, and a very fancy fashion show in the civic center. People park on the streets, in parking lots, and in people's yards. People come every year from all over the country. Many stand for hours just to participate in a piece of history during the enshrinement. Much planning and effort are involved to make this a rousing success. Volunteers are just as numerous and organized as one would find in a major corporation.

THE CONCEPT for a football hall of fame originated in Canton in 1959 when the *Canton Repository* newspaper published an editorial calling for a football hall of fame and that, furthermore, it should be located in Canton. In January 1961, with the backing of city leaders, William E. Umstattd of Timken Steel and Tube Company made a formal proposal to the NFL for the hall of fame to be located in Canton. The bid was accepted three months later, and by February, over $300,000 in pledges was collected for the project. On August 11, 1962, groundbreaking for the hall of fame began as a 19,000-square-foot, two-building complex. Opening of the hall of fame to the public as well as the first-ever hall of fame induction ceremonies were held on September 7, 1963. (Photograph courtesy of the Cleveland Press Collection from Cleveland State University.)

THE PRO FOOTBALL HALL OF FAME has undergone three expansion projects since it opened in 1963. The first one (model seen in this picture) nearly doubled the size of the original hall (34,000 square feet) by adding a third building, which cost $620,000 and was completed on May 10, 1971. In November 1978, a second expansion project was completed that added a fourth building to the complex, costing $1.2 million. The third expansion project, completed on October 1, 1995, added one more building and increased the size of the complex to 83,000 square feet, costing $9.2 million. (Photograph courtesy of the Cleveland Press Collection from Cleveland State University.)

THE PRO FOOTBALL HALL OF FAME has something for everyone, whether it is the casual football fan or football fanatic. The hall tells not only the history of the NFL but of other leagues as well, such as the All-American Football Conference. It contains impressive memorabilia from all areas of the game as well as a gallery honoring the hall of fame inductees. There is also a turntable theater that displays football action on a 20-by-42-foot screen, exhibits that change honoring recent accomplishments in the NFL, interactive games, a snack bar, and a gift shop. (Photographs courtesy of the Cleveland Press Collection from Cleveland State University.)

SIGNS TO THE Pro Football Hall of Fame are located prominently on Interstate 77 in both the northbound and southbound directions. There are also signs along less populated roads, all leading to the most complete collection of professional football history.

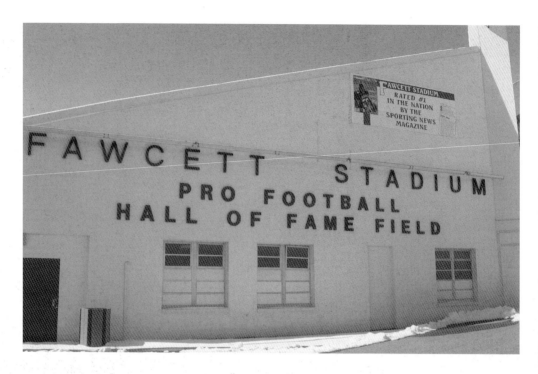

THE PRO FOOTBALL HALL OF FAME Field at Fawcett Stadium, located across the street from the Pro Football Hall of Fame, was built from 1937 to 1939 at an estimated cost of $500,000. Named originally Fawcett Stadium, after former Canton Board of Education member and athlete John A. Fawcett, it originally held 15,000 people and at the time was the largest high school stadium in the country.

FAWCETT FIELD hosted the first hall of fame game on August 11, 1962, between the New York Giants and St. Louis Cardinals (21-21 tie). To accommodate press coverage of the hall of fame games, a $90,000 press box was added to the stadium in 1974. The lower deck of the press box can house up to 73 people to cover games. The upper deck includes four broadcast booths (one television, three radio). The roof of the structure contains a state-of-the-art photo deck. When the hall of fame game started being broadcast at night in 1998, five more light poles were added to the stadium (a total of nine) courtesy of the NFL for $365,000.

In 1997, FAWCETT STADIUM underwent a huge renovation project for $4.3 million. Improvements made to the stadium included the addition of an Astroturf field, new locker rooms, state-of-the-art scoreboards, as well as new lighting and sound systems. Structural repairs were also done to the stadium along with updates made to the press box. As part of the project, the name of the stadium was changed to The Pro Football Hall of Fame Field at Fawcett Stadium.

THE PRO FOOTBALL HALL OF FAME

PRESENTLY, THE PRO FOOTBALL Hall of Fame Field at Fawcett Stadium holds 22,875, which includes 1,500 standing-room-only tickets. The field is the home of three Canton High School teams (Canton McKinley Bulldogs, Timken Trojans, and Plain Local's Glen Oak) and two area colleges (Walsh University and Malone College). The field is also the home of the annual Pro Football Hall of Fame game, which has been held there every year since 1962 (excluding 1966) to start the NFL exhibition season.

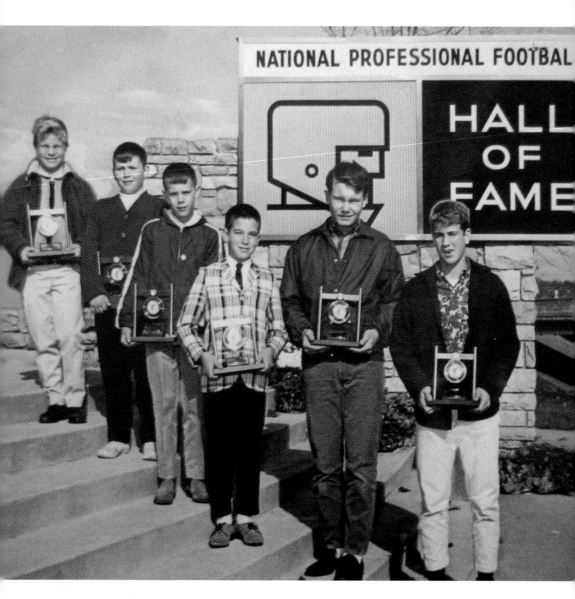

THE PUNT, PASS AND KICK competition started in the 1960s and is today one of the most favorite and famous youth athletic competitions open to both boys and girls from the age of 8 to 15. Winners from local competitions compete on a national level, where a champion is crowned based on age group and gender. The winners of the district competition in 1966 are seen in this picture. From left to right are Mark O'Connell, Gary Satyshur, James Skibbens, Ricky Sherman, Jack Juron, and David Mooney. (Photograph courtesy of the Cleveland Press Collection from Cleveland State University.)

LOU "THE TOE" GROZA (right) was one of the most enduring players of his generation. He played football for 21 years, all with the Cleveland Browns, and was the last one of the 1946 championship team to retire (in 1967). Born in Martins Ferry, Ohio, Groza attended the Ohio State University before joining the Browns in 1946 as an offensive tackle and kicker. He won the 1946 championship game over the Los Angeles Rams 30-28 on a last-second 16-yard field goal to give Paul Brown his first professional football championship. After sitting out the 1960 season with a back injury, Groza returned to the Browns in 1961 as a kicker only. He was chosen as the NFL Player of the Year in 1964, All-NFL tackle for six years, and was elected to nine Pro Bowls. In 21 seasons, he scored 1,608 points, a record that stood for years, and played in four AAFC championship games (winning all 4) and nine NFL championship games (winning 3). He was inducted into the Pro Football Hall of Fame in 1974. (Photograph courtesy of the Cleveland Press Collection from Cleveland State University.)

CHUCK NOLL (No. 65, dark jersey) delivered the Pittsburgh Steelers from the laughing stock of the NFL to four-time Super Bowl champions in the 1970s. Noll was born on January 5, 1932, in Cleveland and attended Benedictine High School in Cleveland. After college at Dayton University, Noll played for the Cleveland Browns from 1953 to 1959 as a guard and linebacker. Following assistant head coaching positions with the Los Angeles/San Diego Chargers and the Baltimore Colts, Noll joined the Pittsburgh Steelers in 1969 as head coach. With an emphasis on the college draft, Noll won nine AFC Central titles and four Super Bowls (IX, X, XIII, and XIV) from 1969 to 1991. He had a career record of 209-156-1 and an impressive 16-8-0 playoff record. He was inducted into the Pro Football Hall of Fame in 1993. (Photograph courtesy of the Cleveland Press Collection from Cleveland State University.)

FULLBACK JIM BROWN (No. 32, dark jersey) is the standard running back to which all Cleveland Browns backs are compared. Born in St. Simons, Georgia, on February 17, 1936, he was the Browns' first-round draft pick out of Syracuse University in 1957. In nine seasons with the Browns (where he never missed a game), Brown gained 12,312 rushing yards, 15,459 combined net yards, and 756 total points. He was elected to the Pro Bowl in all nine years of his career, was first-team All-NFL eight times, was Rookie of the Year in 1957, and was MVP of the NFL in 1958 and 1965. Brown was elected to the Pro Football Hall of Fame in 1971. In 2006, he is a special team consultant to the Cleveland Browns. (Photograph courtesy of the Cleveland Press Collection from Cleveland State University.)

ACROSS AMERICA, PEOPLE ARE DISCOVERING
SOMETHING WONDERFUL. *THEIR HERITAGE.*

Arcadia Publishing is the leading local history publisher in the United States. With more than 3,000 titles in print and hundreds of new titles released every year, Arcadia has extensive specialized experience chronicling the history of communities and celebrating America's hidden stories, bringing to life the people, places, and events from the past. To discover the history of other communities across the nation, please visit:

www.arcadiapublishing.com

Customized search tools allow you to find regional history books about the town where you grew up, the cities where your friends and family live, the town where your parents met, or even that retirement spot you've been dreaming about.